UKE CAN DO IT 2!

UKE CAN DO IT 2!

CLASSROOM UKULELE METHOD

Philip Tamberino

Published in partnership with the
National Association for Music Education

ROWMAN & LITTLEFIELD
Lanham • Boulder • New York • London

Published in cooperation with the National Association for Music Education,
1806 Robert Fulton Drive, Reston, Virginia 20191; nafme.org

Published by Rowman & Littlefield
A wholly owned subsidiary of The Rowman & Littlefield Publishing Group, Inc.
4501 Forbes Boulevard, Suite 200, Lanham, Maryland 20706
www.rowman.com

Unit A, Whitacre Mews, 26-34 Stannary Street, London SE11 4AB, United Kingdom

British Library Cataloguing in Publication Information Available

Library of Congress Cataloging-in-Publication Data

Library of Congress Control Number: 2016939614

♾™ The paper used in this publication meets the minimum requirements of American
National Standard for Information Sciences—Permanence of Paper for Printed Library
Materials, ANSI/NISO Z39.48-1992.

Printed in the United States of America

To the Student

Welcome to the world of making music with the ukulele!

This book will help you learn how to play the ukulele and also how to read and understand music. If you can complete this book you will not only be a better ukulele player but also a better musician!

Some music in this book is just for the ukulele, while other music includes a singing part. Singing and playing at the same time can be tricky for beginners, but if you concentrate on your singing first you'll have an easier time adding the ukulele.

You might move very fast through one part of this book but need more time with another. Everyone is different, but with the right kind of practice, you can improve at anything, and you will.

"Uke" can do it!

Contents

Put a check in the box next to each item you learn:

LEVEL 1

Notes	Chords	Musical Symbols		Songs
☐ g	(none)	☐ Quarter Note	☐ Staff	☐ "Star Light, Star Bright"
☐ c		☐ Quarter Rest	☐ Repeat Sign	☐ "Rain, Rain, Go Away"
☐ e		☐ Music End	☐ G (Treble) Clef	☐ "Ring Around the Rosie"
☐ a		☐ Time Signature	☐ Half Note	
		☐ Bar Line	☐ Half Rest	

LEVEL 2

Notes	Chords	Musical Symbols	Songs	
☐ d	☐ C7	☐ Chord Diagram	☐ "Coconut"	☐ "I Gotta Feeling"
☐ high c	☐ C major	☐ Strum	☐ "Feelin' Alright"	☐ "Duerme Pronto"
	☐ Fsus2	☐ Dotted Half Note	☐ "Exodus"	☐ "Merrily We Roll"
	☐ A minor	☐ Whole Note	☐ "Stand By Me"	☐ "Camptown Races"
		☐ Whole Rest		

LEVEL 3

Notes	Chords	Musical Symbols	Songs	
☐ f	☐ F major	☐ Left Repeat Sign	☐ "Deep in the Heart of Texas"	☐ "Twinkle, Twinkle, Little Star"
☐ b	☐ G7	☐ 1st / 2nd Ending	☐ "Iko Iko"	☐ "When the Saints Go Marching In"
		☐ Eighth Note	☐ "Reggae Got Soul"	☐ "London Bridge"
		☐ Eighth Rest	☐ "Bo Diddley"	☐ "Go Tell Aunt Rhody"
			☐ "Jambalaya (On the Bayou)"	☐ "Merrily We Roll"
			☐ "Mustang Sally"	☐ "Brahms' Lullaby"
			☐ "Lava"	

LEVEL 4

Notes	Chords	Musical Symbols	Songs	
☐ b-flat	☐ B-flat major	☐ Dotted Quarter Note	☐ " Aloha 'Oe"	☐ "Home on the Range"
	☐ G major	☐ Tie	☐ "Let It Be"	☐ "Alouette"
			☐ "Ho Hey"	☐ "Amazing Grace"
			☐ "You Are My Sunshine"	☐ "Everybody Loves Saturday Night"
			☐ "Happy Birthday to You"	☐ "This Land Is Your Land"

3

LOOK

for these icons throughout the book:

Helpful Hint
If you're having trouble, look for this sign

Challenging Question
If you can answer this, you are ready to go on!

Play by Ear
You can play this without reading music

Watch Out!
If you focus on this, you might avoid a common mistake

 Play Along!

with these tracks as you learn the chords

Page	Title	Performer(s)	Album
21	Drifting Blues	B.B. King	Mardi Gras Blues Classics
24	Coconut	Harry Nilsson	Nilsson Schmilsson
26	Feelin' Alright	Joe Cocker	With a Little Help from My Friends
26	You Can't Always Get What You Want	The Rolling Stones	The Rolling Stones Singles Collection
27	Exodus	Bob Marley	Legend
33	Deep in the Heart of Texas	Moe Bandy	A Taste of Texas
33	Iko Iko	Cowboy Mouth	Mardi Gras
33	Reggae Got Soul	311	Surf's Up (Music from the motion picture)
34	Bo Diddley	Bo Diddley	The Chess Box
34	Jambalaya (On the Bayou)	Hank Williams	The Complete Hank Williams
35	Mustang Sally	Wilson Pickett	The Wicked Pickett
36	Lava	Kuana Torres Kahele & Napua Greig	Lava (from "Lava"--short film)
47	This Land Is Your Land	Flatt & Scruggs	Folk Songs of Our Land
47	You Are My Sunshine	Willie Nelson	One for the Road
52	Ho Hey	The Lumineers	The Lumineers
54	Let It Be	The Beatles	Let It Be

The Ukulele

From: Hawaii, USA

Born: Sometime in the 1880s, Kingdom of Hawai'i

Creators: Manuel Nunes, Augusto Dias,
         & Jose do Espirito Santo

Family: String

Close Relatives: Guitar
                     Machete (Portugal)
                     Rajao (Portugal)
                     Cavaquinho (Brazil)
                     Cuatro (Venezuela)

Did You Know?

- ✧ The Hawaiian word *'ukulele* is pronounced "oo-koo-LEH-leh."

- ✧ Ukuleles come in many different shapes, sizes, and colors.

- ✧ The inventors of the ukulele were Portuguese, not Hawaiian.

- ✧ The ukulele was once more popular than the guitar in America.

- ✧ You can play over 20 notes and 100 different chords with the ukulele.

A Ukulele Playlist

✧ Look for these video or audio recordings for a sample of different music featuring the ukulele:

♫ "Somewhere Over the Rainbow /
What a Wonderful World"
performed by **Israel Kamakawiwo'ole**

♫ "Super Mario Theme (live)"
performed by **James Hill**

♫ "Flight of the Bumblebee"
performed by **The Langley Ukulele Ensemble**

♫ "Crazy G (live)"
performed by **Jake Shimabukuro**

♫ "Hey Soul Sister"
performed by **Train**

♫ "I'm Yours"
performed by **Uke3453**

Parts of the ukulele

Knowing these names will make it easier to follow directions and ask questions when learning how to play.

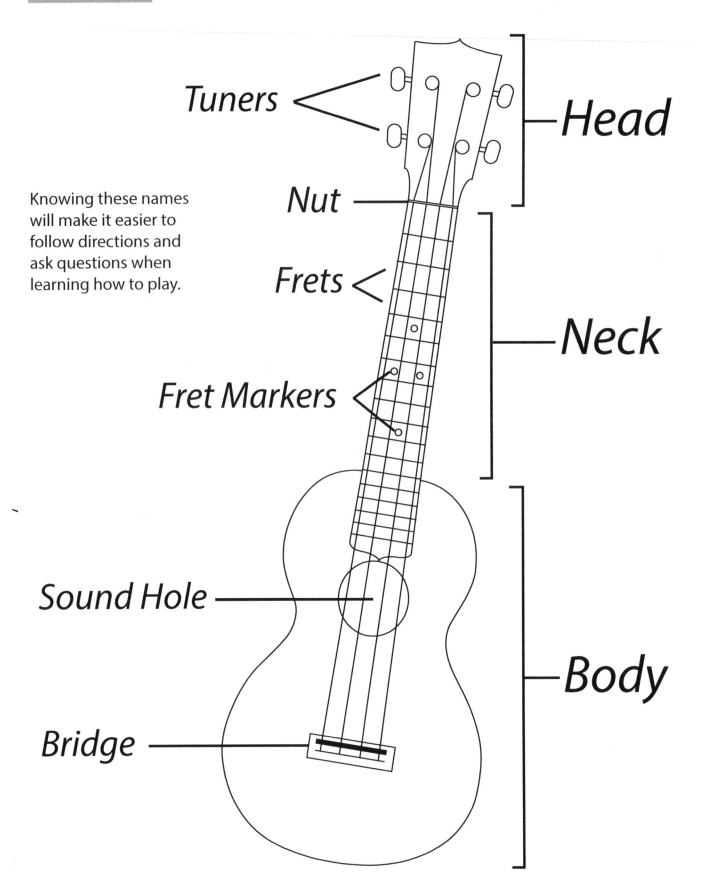

Tuners

Head

Nut

Frets

Neck

Fret Markers

Sound Hole

Bridge

Body

My Ukulele: _____

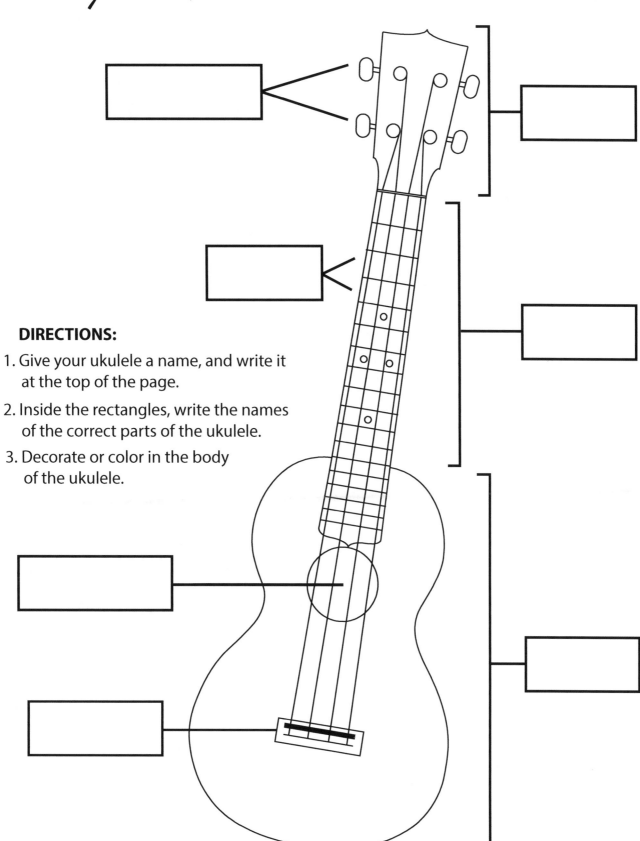

DIRECTIONS:

1. Give your ukulele a name, and write it at the top of the page.

2. Inside the rectangles, write the names of the correct parts of the ukulele.

3. Decorate or color in the body of the ukulele.

How to take care of the ukulele

Keep cases on the floor.
If you have a case, keep it on the floor when taking out the ukulele or putting it away. If it's already on the floor, the ukulele can't fall on the floor by accident.

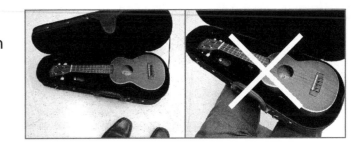

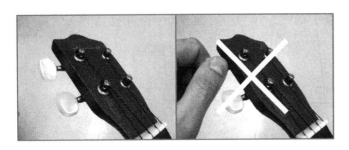

Don't twist the tuners... yet.
It's good if you can tell when your ukulele sounds out of tune, but twisting the tuners can make it worse. Until you learn how to tune the ukulele yourself, give it to your teacher for tuning.

Play on top of the strings.
Grabbing or pulling at the strings when you play slows you down and doesn't make a very good sound. It can also make your ukulele go out of tune faster.

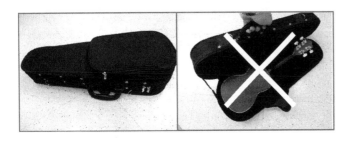

Close the case completely whenever the ukulele is inside.
If the case looks closed, but isn't fastened, your ukulele could fall out on to the floor when you or someone else picks it up.

How to hold the ukulele

Resting Position

- ☑ Body of the ukulele resting face up on your lap

- ☑ Head of the ukulele pointing toward your left

- ☑ Two hands on the ukulele

- ☑ Looking and listening

Ready Position

- ☑ Right forearm pressing the ukulele flat to the middle of your body

- ☑ Right-hand fingers near where the neck and body of the ukulele meet

- ☑ Left arm holding up the neck at about a 45-degree angle

- ☑ Looking and listening

 How will you know when to switch between the resting and ready positions?

 How will you know when to start and stop playing?

How to make a good sound

Strumming with the thumb

☆ This is a soft-sounding strum, using the soft part of your thumb.

☆ Begin at the string closest to your chin, and brush downward, making contact with all strings.

☆ Finish with your thumb toward the floor but near the ukulele.

 Count for four beats, then strum the strings exactly **five times** to the beat and stop.

Picking with the thumb

☆ This is for playing individual notes (only one string at a time).

☆ Push the string downward with the tip of your thumb, then let the string spring back into place.

☆ Finish with your thumb just past the string you picked.

 Count for four beats, then pick the string closest to your chin exactly **five times** to the beat and stop.

Strumming with the pointer finger

☆ This is a louder sounding strum, using the nail of your finger.

☆ With your palm facing your body, point your finger toward yourself.

☆ Brush the tip of your finger across all four strings as you twist your wrist toward the floor.

Learn:

☆ How to play, read, and write the notes **g**, **c**, **e**, and **a**

☆ How to read and use basic musical symbols

☆ How to compose and improvise music

LEVEL 1

Play:

♫ Rain, Rain, Go Away

♫ Ring Around the Rosie

♫ Star Light, Star Bright

and your own compositions!

Getting to know the **OPEN** Strings (g, c, e, a)

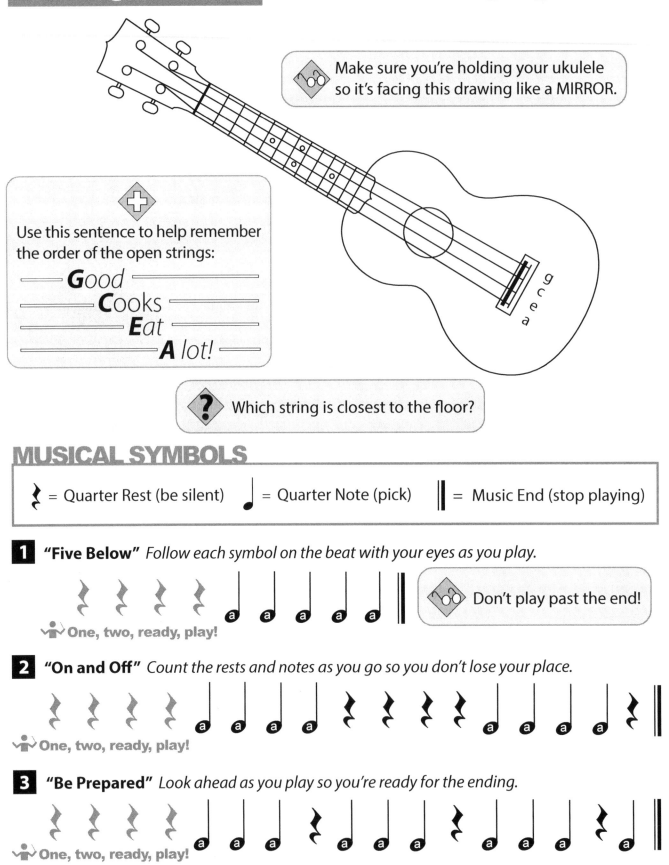

Make sure you're holding your ukulele so it's facing this drawing like a MIRROR.

Use this sentence to help remember the order of the open strings:

Good
Cooks
Eat
A lot!

Which string is closest to the floor?

MUSICAL SYMBOLS

𝄽 = Quarter Rest (be silent)   ♩ = Quarter Note (pick)   𝄂 = Music End (stop playing)

1 **"Five Below"** *Follow each symbol on the beat with your eyes as you play.*

One, two, ready, play!

Don't play past the end!

2 **"On and Off"** *Count the rests and notes as you go so you don't lose your place.*

One, two, ready, play!

3 **"Be Prepared"** *Look ahead as you play so you're ready for the ending.*

One, two, ready, play!

4 **"Easy E"** *Move one string up from **a**, and pick on that string 5 times.*

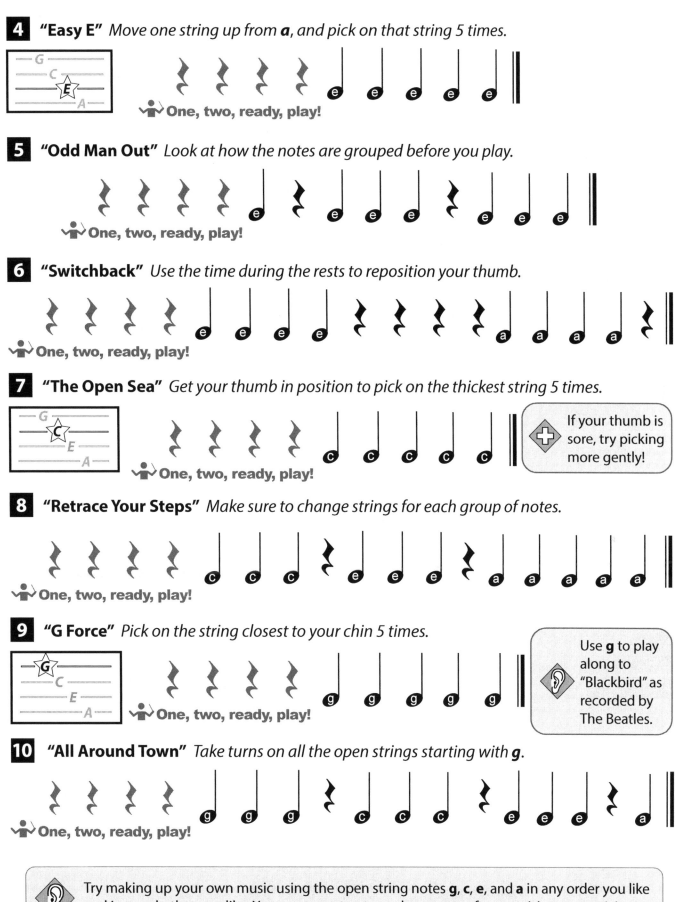

5 **"Odd Man Out"** *Look at how the notes are grouped before you play.*

6 **"Switchback"** *Use the time during the rests to reposition your thumb.*

7 **"The Open Sea"** *Get your thumb in position to pick on the thickest string 5 times.*

If your thumb is sore, try picking more gently!

8 **"Retrace Your Steps"** *Make sure to change strings for each group of notes.*

9 **"G Force"** *Pick on the string closest to your chin 5 times.*

Use **g** to play along to "Blackbird" as recorded by The Beatles.

10 **"All Around Town"** *Take turns on all the open strings starting with **g**.*

 Try making up your own music using the open string notes **g**, **c**, **e**, and **a** in any order you like and in any rhythm you like. You can repeat notes or leave space for rests. It's your music!

MUSICAL SYMBOLS

$\frac{4}{4}$ = 4/4 Time Signature | = Bar Line

≡ = Staff

☆ The **4/4 time signature** means that quarter (1/4) notes and rests will last one beat, and **bar lines** will divide the music into **bars** or **measures** containing exactly **4** beats each.

☆ Writing notes on a **staff** makes it easier to tell notes apart by showing how high or low their pitch is.

11 **"In Time"** *Count four beats at the speed you want to play the notes before playing in 4/4 time.*

 How many measures are in the piece of music above?

12 **"On Staff"** *The circular part of a note is called the "head" and the line is called the "stem."*

13 **"Doubles"** *The note "head" either has a staff line going through it, or it is between two lines.*

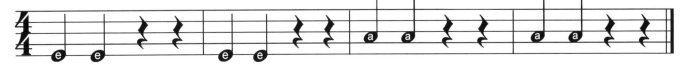

14 **"In 3s"** *How high or low the note head is written on the staff shows us how high or low the pitch is.*

15 **"Upstairs, Downstairs"** *Some notes are so low that we add little extra lines to the staff.*

 Which of the four strings has the highest pitch? Which has the lowest?

14

16 **"Tres Notes"** *Figure out which strings you will use before you begin playing.*

17 **"Keep On Truckin'"** *Read left to right for each line of music until the end.*

Go directly to **e** on the next line!

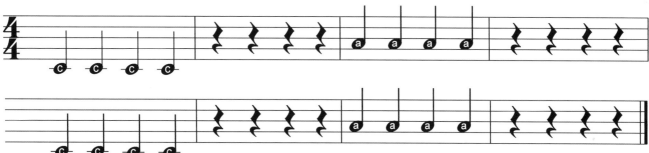

The **time signature** is written once at the beginning but applies to every measure.

18 **"Play It Again, Sam"** *Follow the symbols, even if you recognize how the music sounds.*

MUSICAL SYMBOLS

:|| = Repeat Sign

☆ Seeing a **repeat sign** at the end of a section of music means you should immediately go back to the beginning of the section and play it a second time.

☆ If there is no more music written after the repeat sign, the piece is finished after you repeat it.

19 **"A Shortcut"** *Look for repeat signs before you begin so you are ready when they come up.*

20 **"Same and Different"** *The repeat sign isn't a note or a rest, so it doesn't take up any beats.*

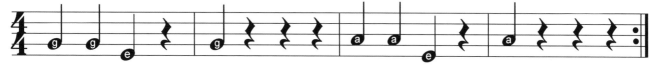

MUSICAL SYMBOLS

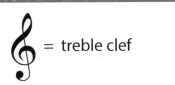
= treble clef

☆ The **treble clef** symbol assigns a specific pitch to each line or space on the staff.

☆ It is also called the **g clef** because the center of the swirl ends by crossing the line used for the note **g**.

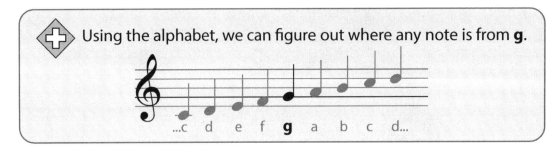

Using the alphabet, we can figure out where any note is from **g**.

...c d e f **g** a b c d...

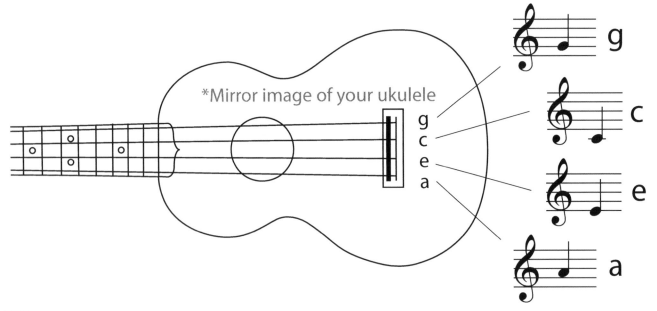

*Mirror image of your ukulele

21 **"What's My Name?"** *Use the diagram to make sure you're playing the correct note.*

22 **"Taking Turns"** *Notes written higher on the staff sound higher than notes written lower.*

Go back to the beginning.

23 **"A Little Lift"** *Each pitch has its own location on the staff.*

16

MUSICAL SYMBOLS

♩ = Half Note   ∎ = Half Rest

☆ **Half notes** last twice as long as quarter notes.

☆ **Half rests** last twice as long as quarter rests.

 If a **quarter note** lasts 1 beat in 4/4 time, how many beats will a **half note** last?

24 **"Stretch It Out"** *Let each half note ring for twice as long as each quarter note.*

25 **"Outside-In"** *The amount of space between the notes doesn't matter, only how each note looks.*

26 **"The Secret Note"** *Always pay attention, even if you think you know what's next.*

27 **"Mystery Melody"** *Finish this famous melody by singing the rest of the line.*

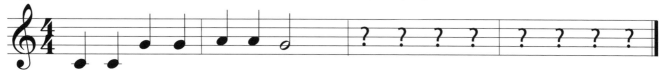

Composing with the open strings

☆ A person who writes music is a **composer**.

☆ Composers use musical symbols the way *authors* use words and punctuation.

DRAWING MUSICAL SYMBOLS

Quarter Note

1. Draw the note head on the staff by coloring in an oval shape.

practice here

2. Draw the stem by starting on the right side above the head and landing on the tip of its side.

practice here

Quarter Rest

1. Draw a capital letter "Z."

practice here

2. Without lifting your pencil, draw a capital "C" underneath the "Z."

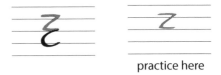

practice here

Music End

1. Color in a thick line that touches the right ends of all the lines of the staff.

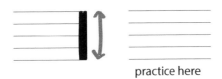

practice here

2. To the left of the thick line, draw a thinner line going from the top line to the bottom.

practice here

☆ Copy the open strings written as quarter notes below:

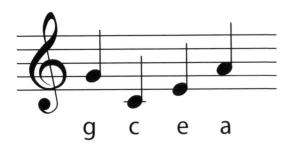

g   c   e   a

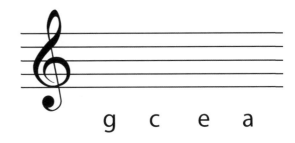

g   c   e   a

1. Write a melody lasting **8 beats** on the staff below using only the open strings (g, c, e, a).

> Print <u>neatly</u> so other people can read what you wrote!

> Use the end symbol.

> **?** Do you know how to play all of the notes you wrote? Try it!

2. Try a different 8-beat-long melody here, and be ready to pass it to someone else to play:

> **+** **Rests** are a natural part of music, like commas or periods in a sentence.

3. Write a **16-beat** long melody here, and use the second line if you run out of room.

4. Write a melody using the open strings that fits the **time signature**.

19

Singing & Playing with the open strings

g c e a

Check here to make sure you're playing the right pitches!

28 **"Star Light, Star Bright"** *Sing this song first, then try playing it (use only two strings!).*

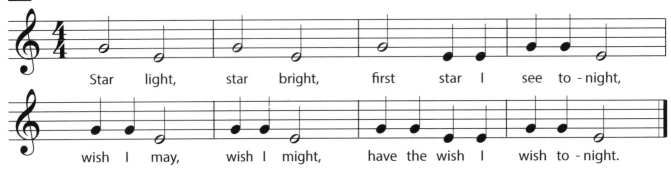

Star light, star bright, first star I see to - night,

wish I may, wish I might, have the wish I wish to - night.

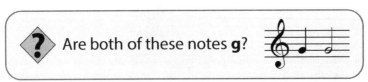
Are both of these notes **g**?

29 **"Rain, Rain, Go Away"** *Look at which notes are used in the piece before you begin playing.*

Rain, rain, go a - way, come a - gain a - no - ther day.

We want to go out and play. Rain, rain, go a - way.

30 **"Ring Around the Rosie"** *If you have trouble playing and singing, just sing!*

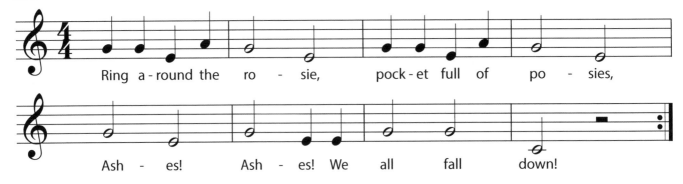

Ring a - round the ro - sie, pock - et full of po - sies,

Ash - es! Ash - es! We all fall down!

20

Improvising with the open strings

☆ Any time you make something up without exactly planning it ahead of time you are **improvising**. When you improvise music, *you* get to choose which notes to play and when.

☆ When playing certain styles of music with other people, it is common for everybody to play a written part at the beginning together and then *take turns* improvising.

☆ It is important to *look* and *listen* to other people when playing together, so you will be able to know when it's your turn and when your turn is finished.

Not sure what to play? Here are **5** things you can do when improvising:

1. Try notes in different orders

2. Try different rhythms

3. Repeat the same note when you like

4. Take rests when you like

5. Listen to other musicians for ideas

 You can use the open strings to improvise along with "Drifting Blues" as recorded by B.B. King.

31 **"12-Bar Blues in A"** *You can play this pattern together before taking turns improvising*

 What does the number **12** refer to in the title of this piece?

Learn:

✰ How to read chord symbols and strum symbols

✰ How to play the chords **C7**, **C major**, **Fsus2**, and **A minor**

✰ How to play, read, and write the notes **d** and **high c**

✰ How to play the C major pentatonic scale

LEVEL 2

Play:

♫ Camptown Races

♫ Coconut

♫ Duerme Pronto

♫ Exodus

♫ Feelin' Alright

♫ I Gotta Feeling

♫ Stand by Me

♫ You Can't Always Get What You Want

How to Read Chord Diagrams

☆ We can create a diagram to symbolize the strings and first four frets of the ukulele:

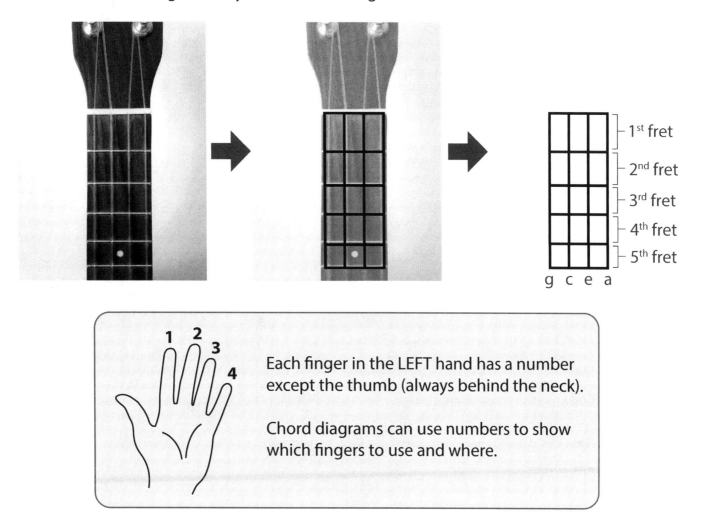

Each finger in the LEFT hand has a number except the thumb (always behind the neck).

Chord diagrams can use numbers to show which fingers to use and where.

☆ We can put black dots on the diagram to symbolize where to press, and with which finger:

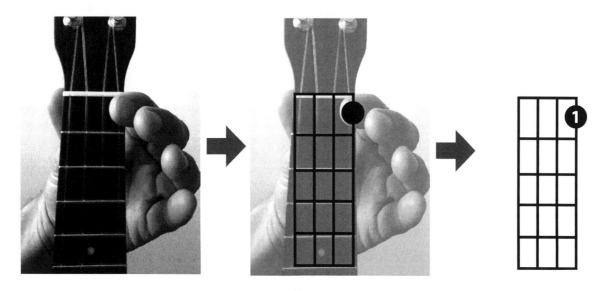

☆ When we see a **chord name** written above the diagram, it means that if we put our fingers where the diagram tells us, we can hear that chord by strumming with the other hand.

C7

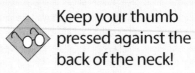
Keep your thumb pressed against the back of the neck!

➡️ **Strum!**

You can use the C7 chord to play along to the song "Coconut," as recorded by Harry Nilsson. Just press ▷ and strum along!

MUSICAL SYMBOLS

 = Slash

☆ A slash represents one beat but does not tell us which notes to play.

☆ We can write chord diagrams above the staff and strum them on every beat we see a slash.

32 **"Four Plus One"** *Instead of counting the strums, count the beats in each measure.*

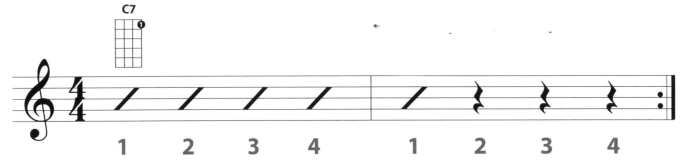

33 **"Air Strum"** *When you see a rest, strum in the air in front of the strings.*

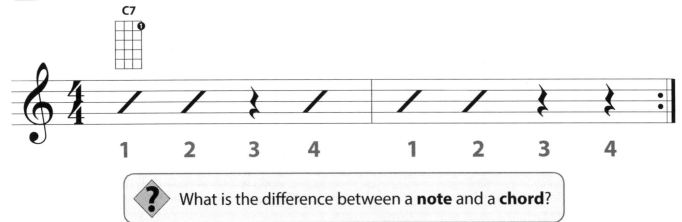

? What is the difference between a **note** and a **chord**?

24

C major

New Chord!

The strings will not hurt you, but your fingertips might feel a little sore at first.

You can sing many songs while strumming the C major chord on the beat. Try *"Frère Jacques,"* "Three Blind Mice," or "Row, Row, Row Your Boat."

34 **"March"** *This strumming pattern will also work for any of the songs mentioned above.*

35 **"Change Up"** *Use the time during rests to get your finger in place for the next chord.*

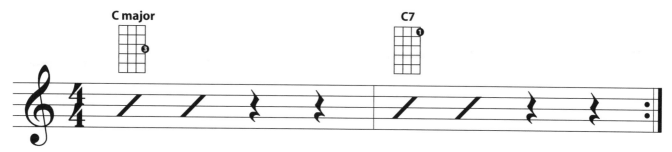

When fretting strings, keep any unused fingers close to the fretboard so they are not very far away when it's time to use them.

36 **"Wait For It"** *Not all music begins with sound on the first beat of the measure.*

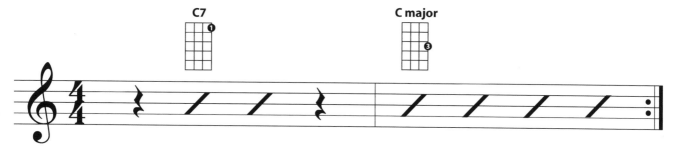

Fsus2

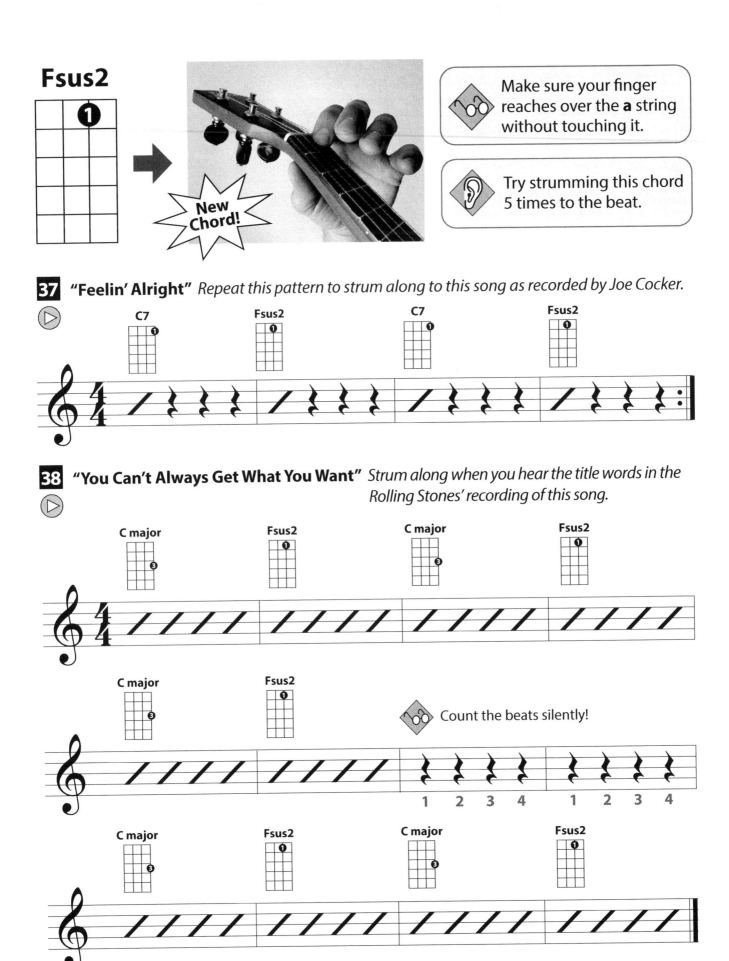

New Chord!

Make sure your finger reaches over the **a** string without touching it.

Try strumming this chord 5 times to the beat.

37 **"Feelin' Alright"** *Repeat this pattern to strum along to this song as recorded by Joe Cocker.*

C7   Fsus2   C7   Fsus2

38 **"You Can't Always Get What You Want"** *Strum along when you hear the title words in the Rolling Stones' recording of this song.*

C major   Fsus2   C major   Fsus2

C major   Fsus2

Count the beats silently!

1 2 3 4   1 2 3 4

C major   Fsus2   C major   Fsus2

A minor

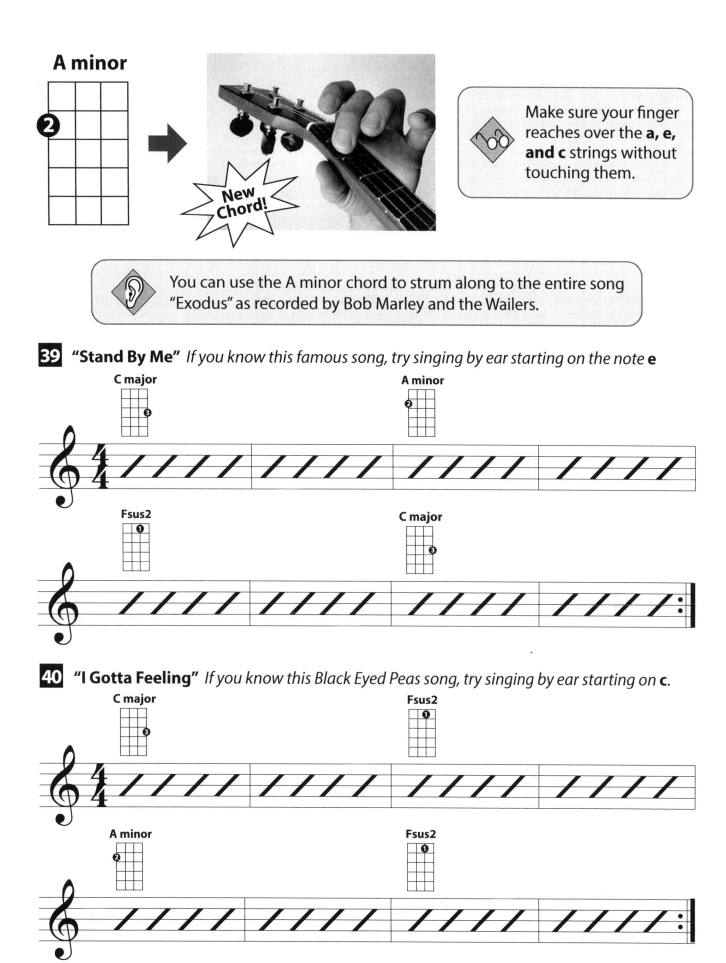

New Chord!

Make sure your finger reaches over the **a, e, and c** strings without touching them.

You can use the A minor chord to strum along to the entire song "Exodus" as recorded by Bob Marley and the Wailers.

39 **"Stand By Me"** *If you know this famous song, try singing by ear starting on the note* **e**

C major

A minor

Fsus2

C major

40 **"I Gotta Feeling"** *If you know this Black Eyed Peas song, try singing by ear starting on* **c**.

C major

Fsus2

A minor

Fsus2

27

Getting to know the note **d**

☆ We can use a chord diagram to show how to play a **note** by putting an "x" over unused strings.

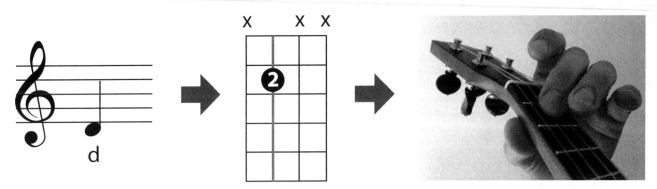

d

> 🎵 Be sure not to strum all strings. Your right thumb should pick the one string that your left hand is fretting.

41 **"Under and Over"** *Keep your finger pressed on **d** through the whole piece.*

42 **"Going Lower"** *The lower notes in this piece share the same string.*

43 **"Let it Ring"** *Each different note in this piece uses a different string.*

44 **"Duerme Pronto"** *Sing the lyrics in English or Spanish. Try the other when you repeat.*

Duer - me pron - to, ni - ño lin - do, duer - me pron - to, sin llo - rar.
Go to sleep now, lit - tle ba - by, go to sleep now, don't you cry.

45 **"Merrily We Roll"** *Keep your fretting fingers close to the fretboard even when not in use*

Mer - ri - ly we roll a - long, roll a - long, roll a - long

Mer - ri - ly we roll a - long, o'er the deep blue sea.

MUSICAL SYMBOLS

 = Dotted half note

☆ **Dotted half notes** last as long as 3 quarter notes.

? If a **quarter note** lasts 1 beat in 3-4 time, how many beats will a **dotted half note** last?

46 **"Camptown Races"** *You can use different fingers for picking different strings*

Camp-town la - dies sing this song, doo - dah doo - dah . . .

Camp-town race track's five miles long, oh, doo - dah day.

Getting to know the note **high c**

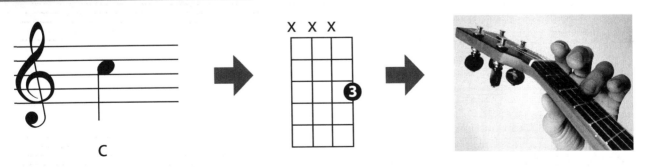

C

x x x
③

+ The note's stem can point down for higher notes.

+ This is the same fingering as the **C major chord**.

⬦ Pick only on the string you are fretting.

47 **"On the High Seas"** *You can keep your 3rd finger on the fretboard during this entire piece.*

48 **"That's So Me"** *Don't move your 3rd finger too far away from the fretboard when not in use.*

Getting to know the **C major pentatonic scale**

☆ A **scale** is a way of organizing a set of notes in order of increasing or decreasing pitch.

☆ The starting note of a scale is always included in the name of the scale.

☆ The lowest and highest notes of a scale always have the same name.

The C major Pentatonic Scale

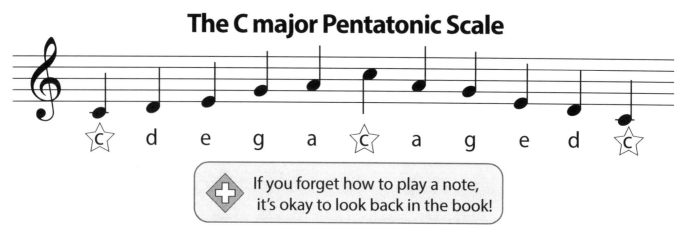

> ✚ If you forget how to play a note, it's okay to look back in the book!

MUSICAL SYMBOLS

𝅝	= Whole Note
▬	= Whole Rest

☆ **Whole notes** last as long as *four* quarter notes.

☆ **Whole rests** last as long as *four* quarter rests.

> **?** If a **quarter note** lasts 1 beat in 4/4 time, how many beats will a **whole note** last?

Try playing the C major pentatonic scale in whole notes:

Now try the scale using dotted quarter notes:

Composing with the C major pentatonic scale

☆ Last time, we wrote music using only quarter notes and quarter rests. This time, try adding some of the other note and rest values we've learned:

DRAWING MUSICAL SYMBOLS

Half Note

1. Draw the note head on the staff as an outlined oval.

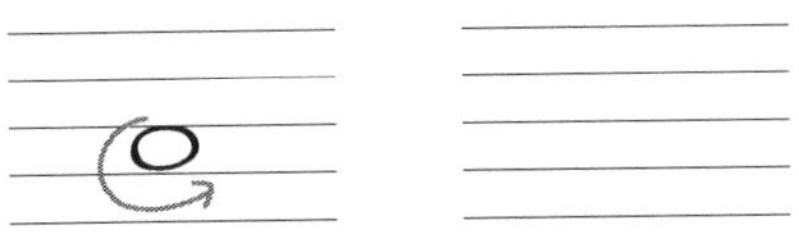

practice here

2. Draw the stem by starting on the right side above the head and landing on the tip of its side.

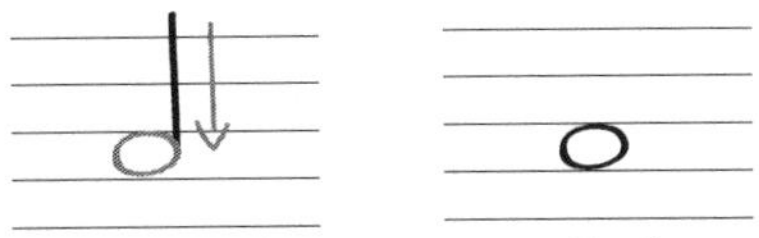

practice here

Half Rest

1. Draw a rectangle sitting on the middle line of the staff.

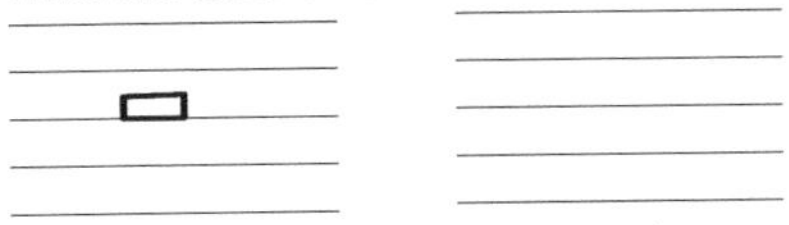

practice here

2. Color in the rectangle.

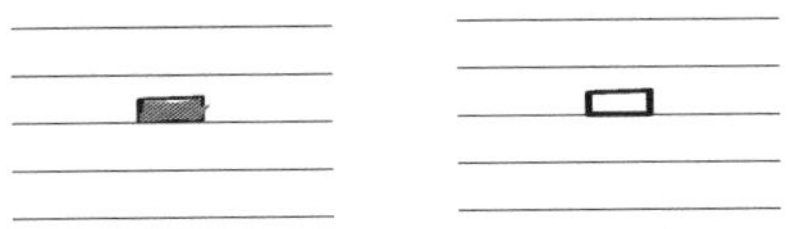

practice here

4/4 Time Signature

1. Draw the number "4" in the top two spaces on the staff.

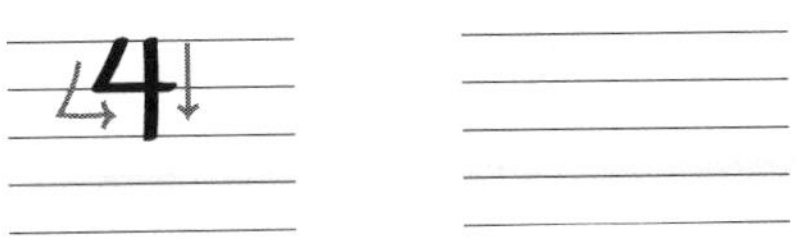

practice here

2. Draw another "4" directly below the other in the bottom two spaces of the staff.

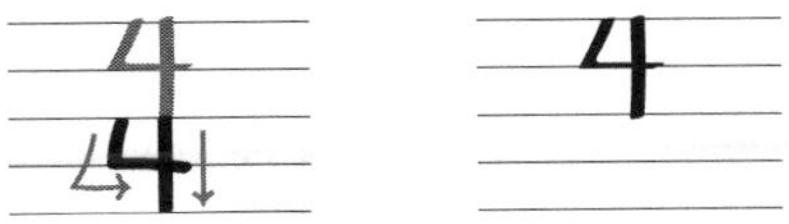

practice here

☆ Write a melody on the staff below using only pitches from the C major pentatonic scale, in 4/4 time.

| Don't forget to write the **time signature!** | Use bar lines to divide the music into equal measures. | Draw the music end symbol at the end! |

Learn:

☆ How to read, play, and write the notes **f** and **b**

☆ How to play the chords **F major** and **G7**

☆ How to play the C major scale

☆ How to read a lead sheet

LEVEL 3

Play:

♫ Deep in the Heart of Texas

♫ Go Tell Aunt Rhody

♫ Iko Iko

♫ Jambalaya (On the Bayou)

♫ Lava

♫ Merrily We Roll

♫ Mustang Sally

♫ Reggae Got Soul

♫ Twinkle, Twinkle, Little Star

♫ When the Saints Go Marching In

F major

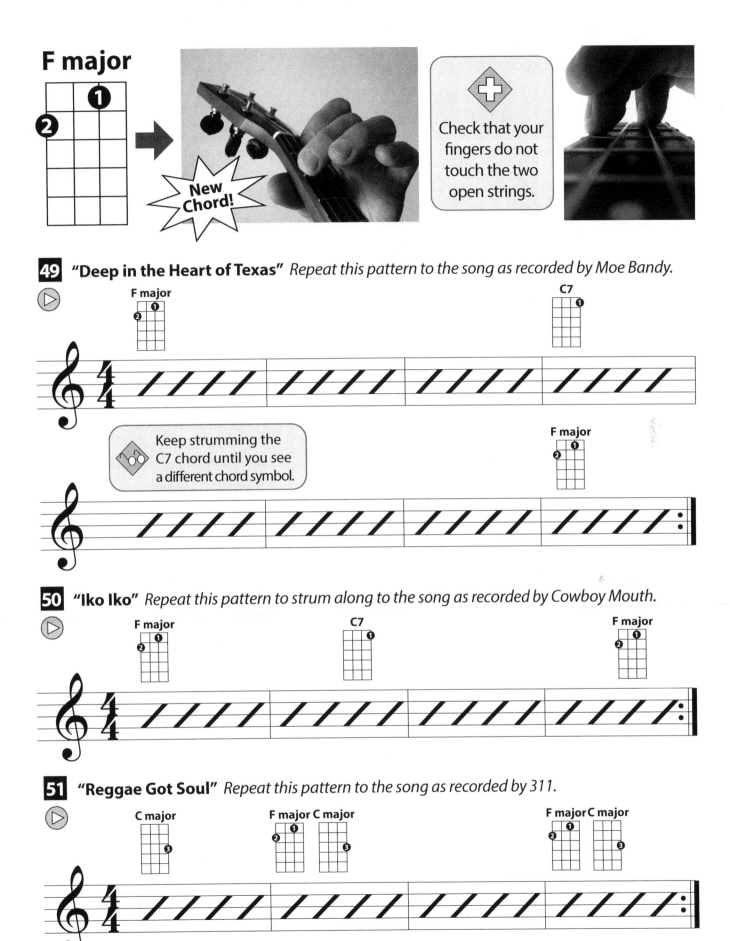

Check that your fingers do not touch the two open strings.

New Chord!

49 **"Deep in the Heart of Texas"** *Repeat this pattern to the song as recorded by Moe Bandy.*

F major

C7

Keep strumming the C7 chord until you see a different chord symbol.

F major

50 **"Iko Iko"** *Repeat this pattern to strum along to the song as recorded by Cowboy Mouth.*

F major

C7

F major

51 **"Reggae Got Soul"** *Repeat this pattern to the song as recorded by 311.*

C major

F major C major

F major C major

G7

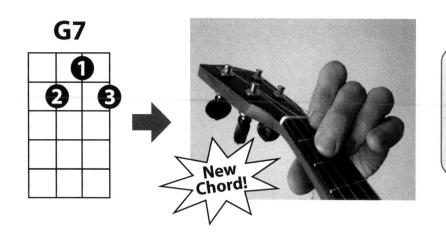

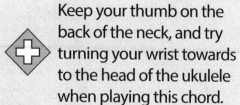

Keep your thumb on the back of the neck, and try turning your wrist towards to the head of the ukulele when playing this chord.

You can play the G7 chord on the beat to the song "Bo Diddley" as recorded by the musician Bo Diddley.

52 **"Bo Diddley Beat"** *A faster version of this pattern is used throughout the song "Bo Diddley."*

53 **"Jambalaya (On the Bayou)"** *Play this pattern along with the song as recorded by Hank Williams.*

Slide your third finger along the **a** string instead of lifting it off when changing chords.

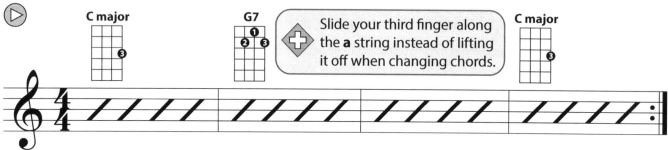

Need more time to change chords? Try strumming only on the beats where you see a new chord symbol. Use the beats in between to get your hand set for the next chord.

MUSICAL SYMBOLS

 = Begin repeat

☆ A **begin repeat** sign (like a regular repeat sign facing backward) signals the beginning of a section you will repeat when you come to a regular repeat sign.

34

54 "Mustang Sally" *Try strumming along to this song as recorded by Wilson Pickett.*

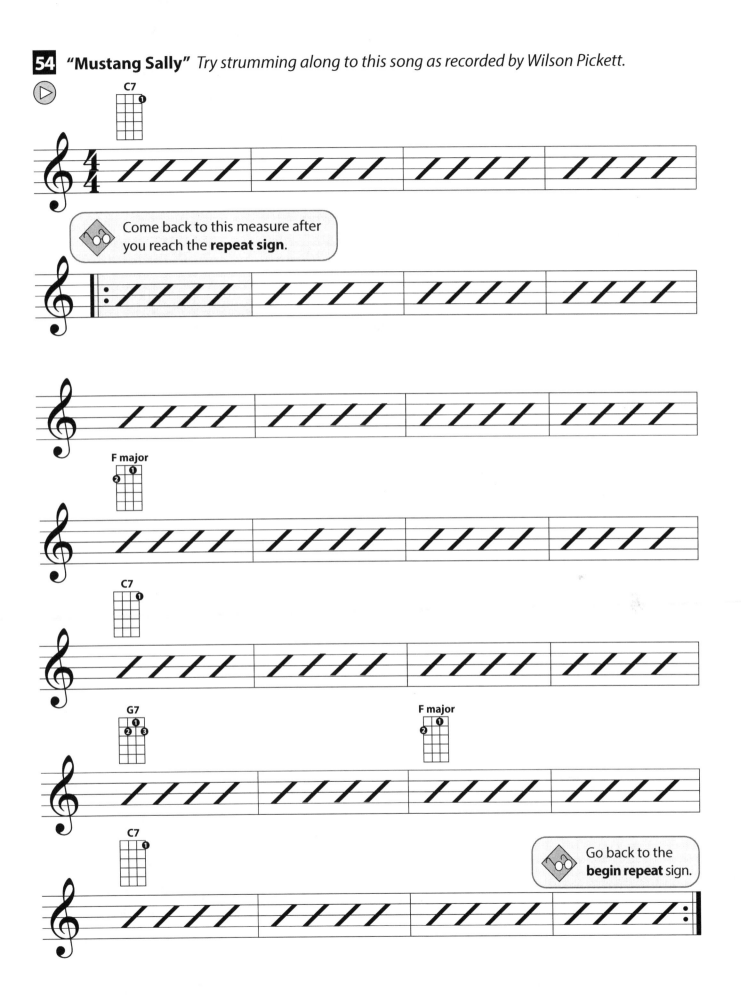

MUSICAL SYMBOLS

1. ▭	= First ending
2. ▭	= Second ending

☆ Sometimes a repeated section of music will have a different ending when played the second time.

☆ The first time you play the section, play only the music under the **first ending** symbol. The second time, skip the first ending and play only the **second ending**.

55 **"Lava"** *Try strumming along to this song from the Disney short film of the same name.*

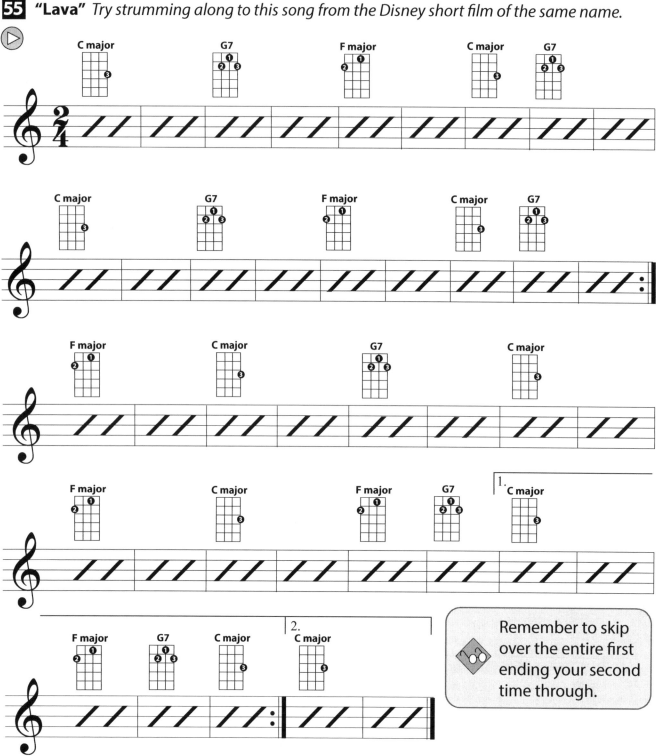

Remember to skip over the entire first ending your second time through.

36

Getting to know the note **f**

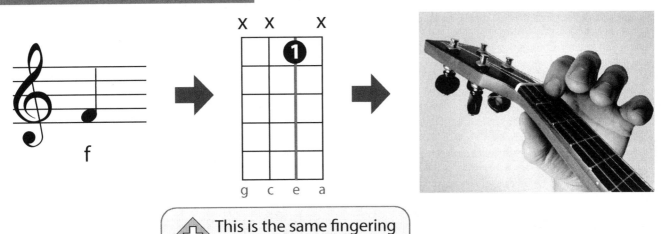

g c e a

✚ This is the same fingering used for the **Fsus2 chord**.

56 **"On and Off"** *Start with your finger ready to play **f**, but release it to play **e**.*

MUSICAL SYMBOLS

♪ = Eighth Note

𝄾 = Eighth Rest

♫ = **Attached eighth notes**

☆ **Eighth notes** last *half as long* as quarter notes.

☆ **Eighth rests** last *half as long* as quarter rests.

☆ We can **attach** eighth notes that are next to each other without changing their length.

? If a **quarter note** lasts 1 beat in 4/4 time, how long does an **eighth note** last?

57 **"Getting Closer"** *Start slow enough to be able to play the shorter notes at the end.*

58 **"Big Ben"** *Each different note in this piece uses a different string.*

59 **"Twinkle, Twinkle, Little Star"** *Try learning one measure at a time, then try longer parts.*

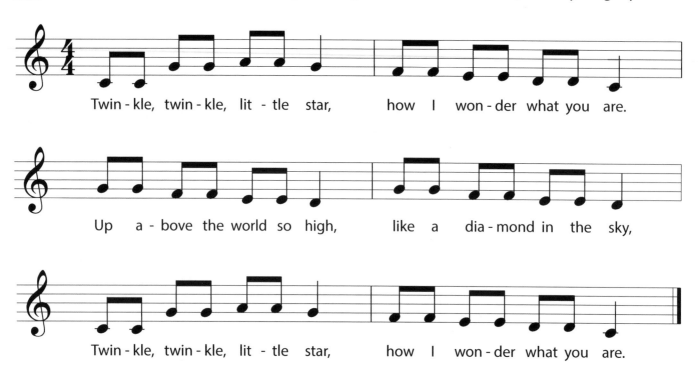

Twin - kle, twin - kle, lit - tle star, how I won - der what you are.

Up a - bove the world so high, like a dia - mond in the sky,

Twin - kle, twin - kle, lit - tle star, how I won - der what you are.

60 **"When the Saints Go Marching In"** *Try learning one line at a time, then try longer parts.*

Oh when the saints go mar - ching in,

oh when the saints go mar - ching in,

oh I want to be in that num - ber

when the saints go mar - ching in.

Getting to know the note **b**

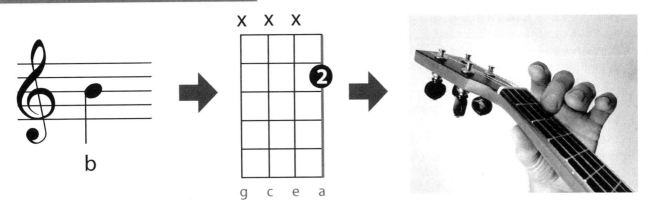

b

x x x

2

g c e a

61 **"Circle Back"** *Remember to use your third (ring) finger when playing* **high c**.

62 **"The New World"** *Keep your fingers close to the fretboard even when not in use.*

63 **"Once Upon a Time"** *Use the time during the whole notes to change fingering.*

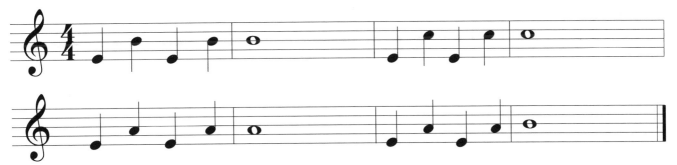

64 **"Jolly Old St. Nicholas"** *This tune uses all four strings. Try two bars at a time at first.*

Getting to know the **C major scale**

☆ When you sing a **major scale** you can use the syllables *do, re, mi, fa, sol, la,* and *ti.*

☆ The C major scale uses every individual note you have learned to play and read so far.

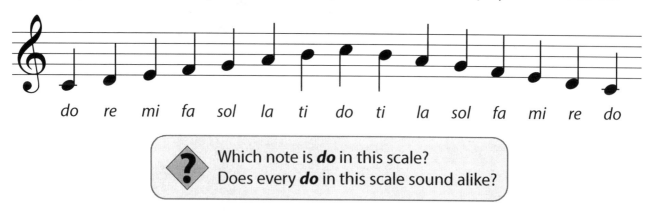

do re mi fa sol la ti do ti la sol fa mi re do

> **?** Which note is **do** in this scale?
> Does every **do** in this scale sound alike?

☆ Try playing the C major scale in whole notes:

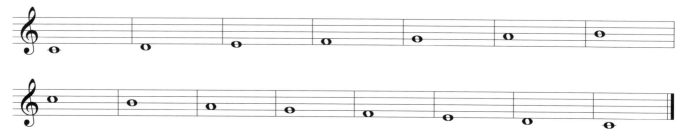

☆ How about playing two **half** notes on each note?

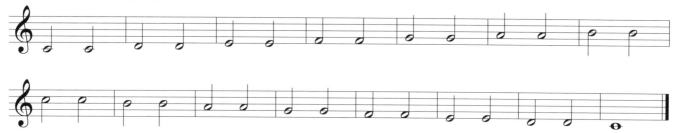

☆ When you're ready, try four **quarter** notes on each note:

Getting to know lead sheets

☆ **Lead sheets** give you the basic instructions for how to play a song, including:

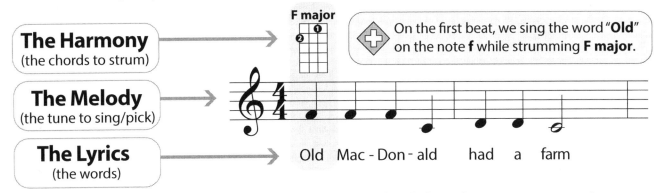

The Harmony
(the chords to strum)

The Melody
(the tune to sing/pick)

The Lyrics
(the words)

F major

On the first beat, we sing the word "**Old**" on the note **f** while strumming **F major**.

Old Mac-Don-ald had a farm

☆ You may strum on every beat or in a pattern—the lead sheet leaves it up to you!

65 **"London Bridge"** *Try singing while picking the melody, then while strumming the harmony.*

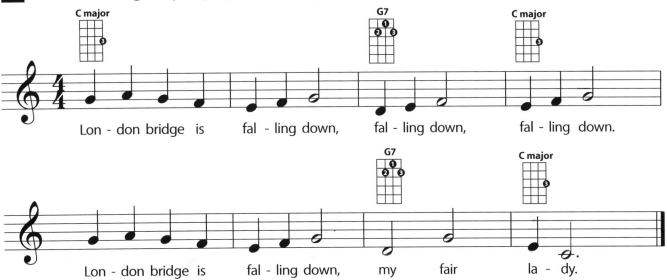

Lon - don bridge is fal - ling down, fal - ling down, fal - ling down.

Lon - don bridge is fal - ling down, my fair la - dy.

66 **"Go Tell Aunt Rhody"** *This song uses the same chord pattern as "London Bridge."*

Go tell Aunt Rho - dy, go tell Aunt Rho ___ - dy,

go tell Aunt Rho - dy the old grey goose is dead.

67 **"Merrily We Roll"** *You tried picking this at level 2, now try strumming while you sing.*

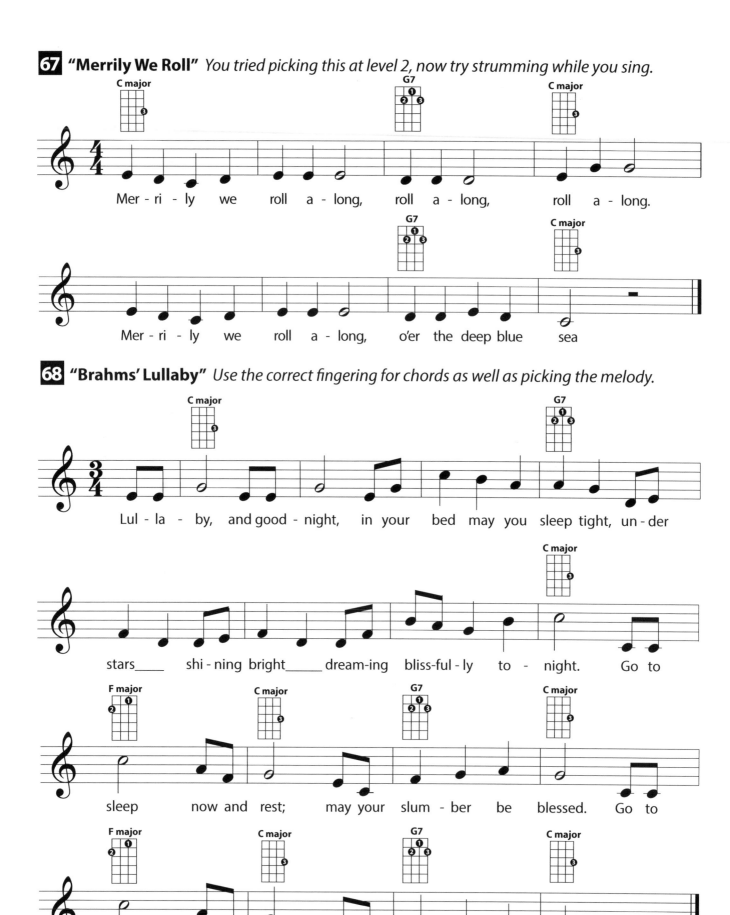

Mer - ri - ly we roll a - long, roll a - long, roll a - long.

Mer - ri - ly we roll a - long, o'er the deep blue sea

68 **"Brahms' Lullaby"** *Use the correct fingering for chords as well as picking the melody.*

Lul - la - by, and good - night, in your bed may you sleep tight, un - der

stars____ shi - ning bright_____ dream-ing bliss-ful - ly to - night. Go to

sleep now and rest; may your slum - ber be blessed. Go to

sleep now and rest; may your slum - ber be blessed.

Learn:

☆ How to read **flat signs**

☆ How to play the chords **B-flat major** and **G major**

☆ How to play the note **b-flat**

☆ How to understand a **key signature**

LEVEL 4

Play:

♫ Aloha 'Oe

♫ Amazing Grace

♫ Everybody Loves Saturday Night

♫ Happy Birthday to You

♫ Ho Hey

♫ Home on the Range

♫ Let It Be

♫ This Land Is Your Land

♫ You Are My Sunshine

Getting to know the note **b-flat**

MUSICAL SYMBOLS

♭ = Flat sign

☆ A **flat sign** changes the name, fingering, and pitch of a note on the staff.

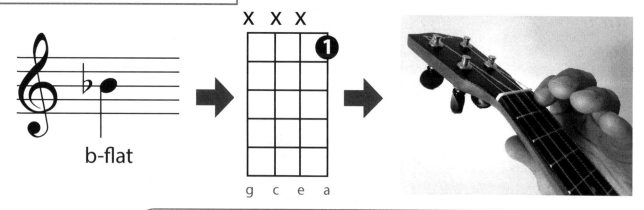

b-flat

g c e a

Which sounds higher in pitch—**b** or **b-flat**?

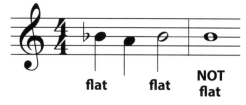

flat   flat   NOT flat

☆ A flat sign next to a note lasts for the rest of the measure without needing to be written again. After the end of the measure, the note goes back to normal.

flat   flat   flat

☆ Flat signs written next to the treble clef symbol last for the *entire line of music* without needing to be written again. This area is called the **key signature**.

69 **"You'll B Fine"** *Keep your fingers close to the fretboard between notes.*

70 **"Round and Round"** *You can leave your 1st finger on **b-flat** while your 3rd plays **c**.*

The flat sign applies to the second **b** too.

71 **"Ambling"** *Keep your fretting fingers close to the strings even when not in use.*

This key signature makes all **b**s flat.

72 **"Everybody Loves Saturday Night"** *Try strumming on the first beat of each measure while you sing.*

F major   C7   F major

Ev - 'ry - bo - dy   loves   Sa - tur - day   night_____

F major   C7   F major

Ev - 'ry - bo - dy   loves   Sa - tur - day   night_____

F major   C7   F major   C7

Ev - 'ry - bo - dy   Ev - 'ry - bo - dy   Ev - 'ry - bo - dy   Ev - 'ry - bo - dy

F major   C7   F major

Ev - 'ry - bo - dy   loves   Sa - tur - day   night_____

MUSICAL SYMBOLS

♩. = Dotted quarter note

☆ **Dotted quarter notes** last one-and-a-half times as long as a regular quarter note.

? If a quarter note lasts one beat in 4/4 time, for how many beats will a dotted quarter note last?

73 **"Alouette"** *You can leave your finger on* **f** *through the first four measures (and the last four too).*

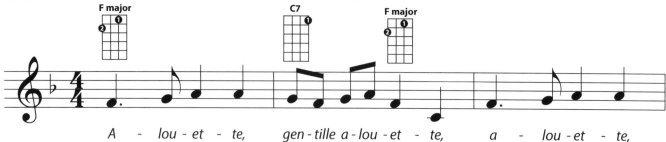

A - lou - et - te,   gen - tille a - lou - et - te,   a - lou - et - te,

je te plu - me - rai!   Je te plu - me - rai la tête,   je te plu - me - rai la tête,

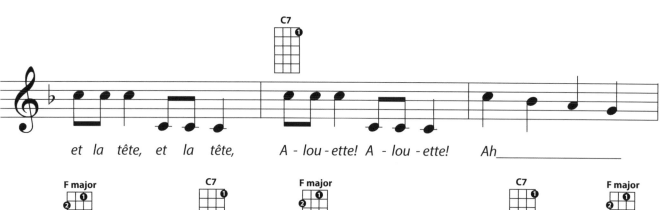

et la tête, et la tête,   A - lou - ette! A - lou - ette!   Ah_____

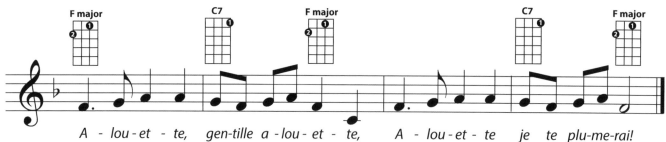

A - lou - et - te,   gen - tille a - lou - et - te,   A - lou - et - te   je te plu - me - rai!

? Should these two melodies sound different? Why or why not?

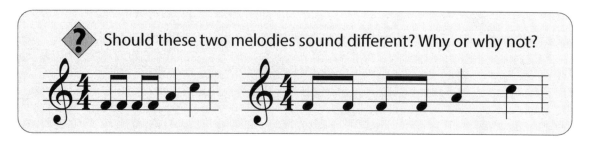

B♭ major

Your first finger presses down on **two strings at the same time** to play this chord.

74 **"This Land Is Your Land"** *You can strum along to the song as recorded by Flatt & Scruggs.*

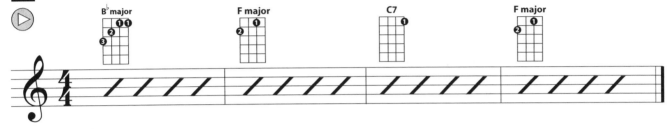

75 **"Happy Birthday to You"** *Who's birthday is today or coming soon?*

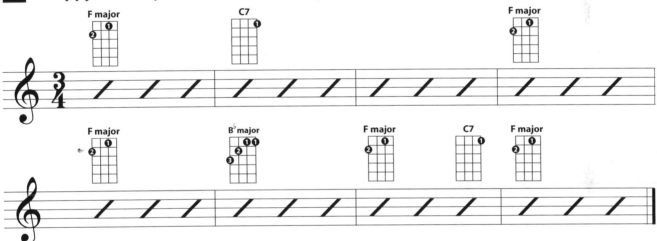

76 **"You Are My Sunshine"** *You can strum along to this song as recorded by Willie Nelson.*

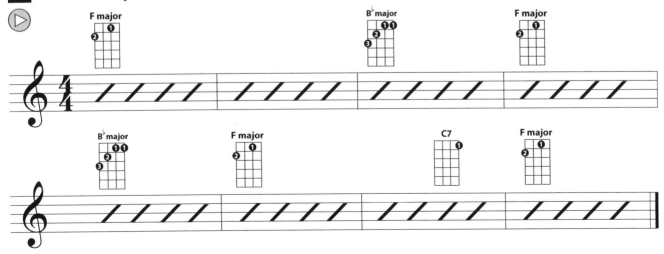

77 **"Aloha 'Oe"** *This famous song was written by the last monarch to rule Hawai'i, Queen Lili'uokalani.*

A - lo - ha 'oe, a - lo - ha 'oe, e -

keo - na - o - na no - ho i ka li - po_____ One

fond em - brace, a hoi ae au, un -

- til we meet a - gain.

78 **"Amazing Grace"** *Use your pointer as well as your thumb to play the eighth notes.*

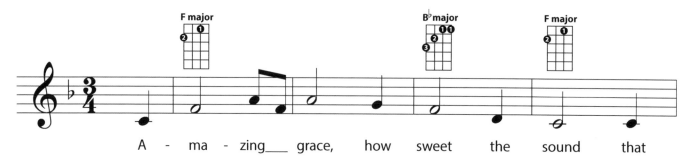

A - ma - zing___ grace, how sweet the sound that

saved a___ wretch like me_____. I

once was___ lost, but now I'm found; was

blind but___ now I see_____.

79 **"Home on the Range"** *Using the proper fingering for each note will help you pick this melody.*

Oh give me a home where the buf - fa - lo roam, where the

deer and the an - te - lope play_____, where

sel - dom is heard a dis - cou - rag - ing word, and the

skies   are   not   clou - dy   all   day_____.

Home,   home   on   the   range_____ ,   where   the

deer   and   the   an - te - lope   play_____ ,   where

sel - dom   is   heard   a   dis - cou - ra - ging   word,   and   the

skies   are   not   clou - dy   all   day_____ ;   and   the

skies   are   not   clou - dy   all   day_____ .

50

G major

New Chord!

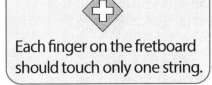

Each finger on the fretboard should touch only one string.

80 **"The End"** *Move your 3rd (ring) finger first as you switch between the chords.*

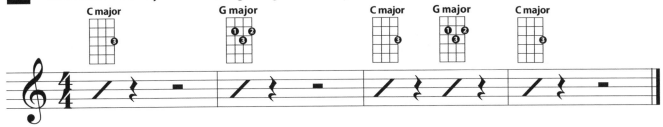

81 **"Ode to Joy"** *Ludwig van Beethoven (1770-1827) wrote this melody without being able to hear.*

51

82 **"Ho Hey"** *Try strumming along to this song as recorded by The Lumineers.*

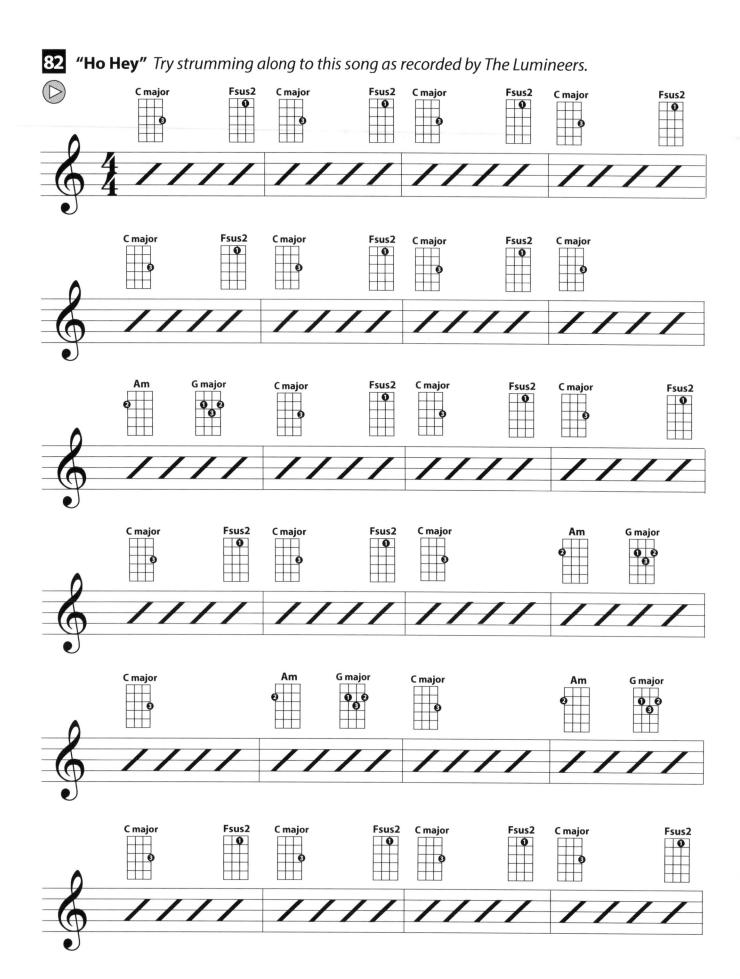

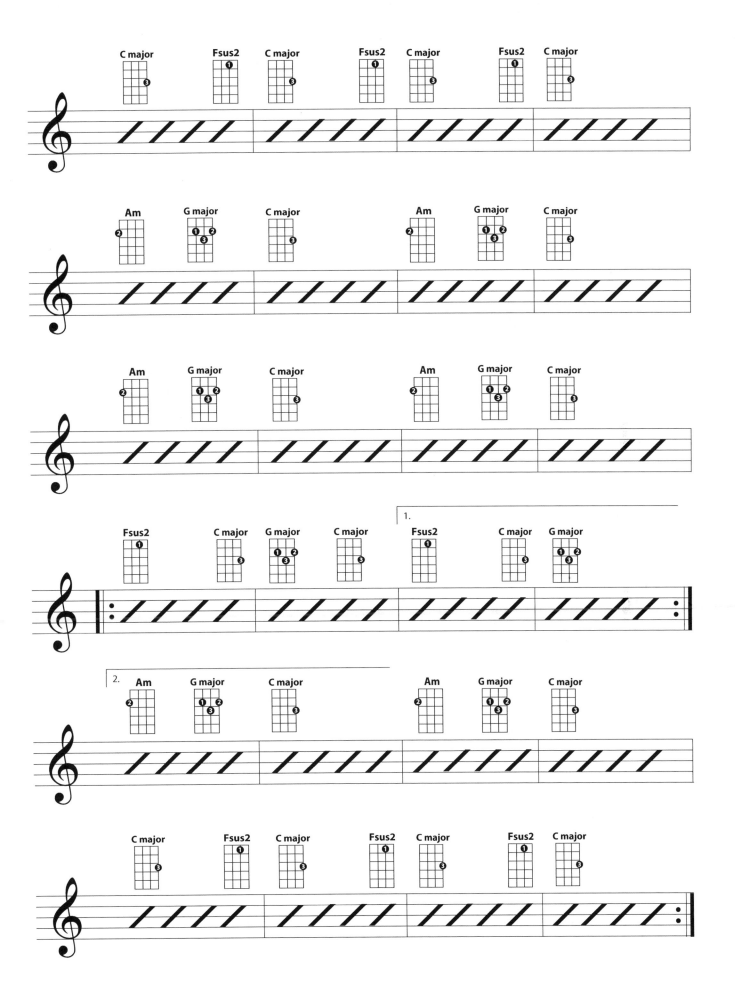

83 **"Let It Be"** *Try strumming along to this song as recorded by The Beatles.*

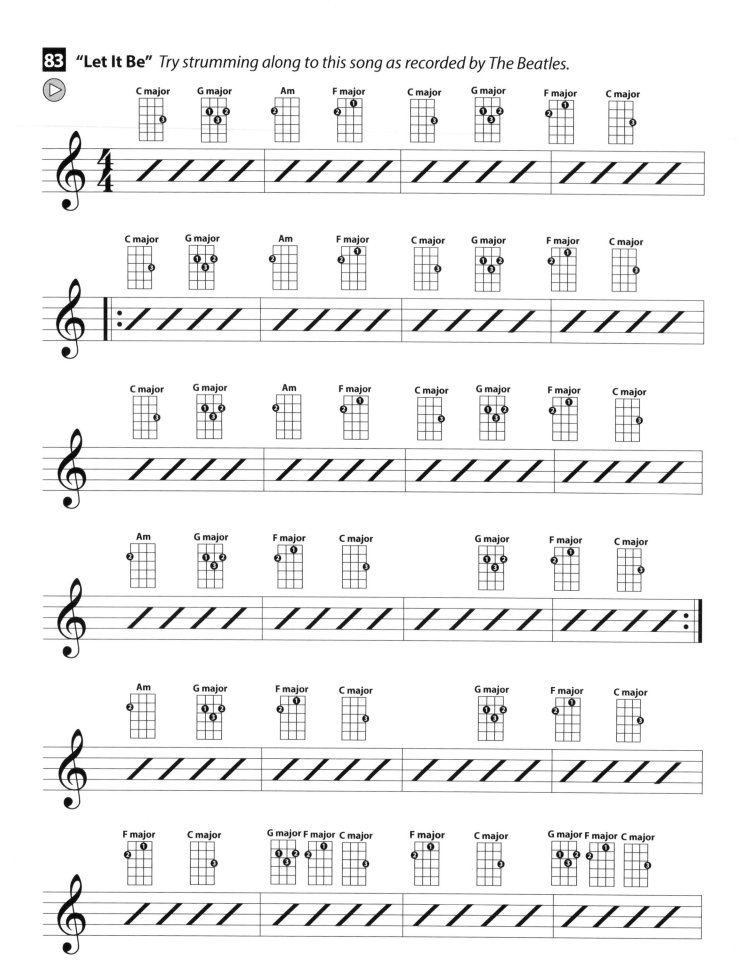

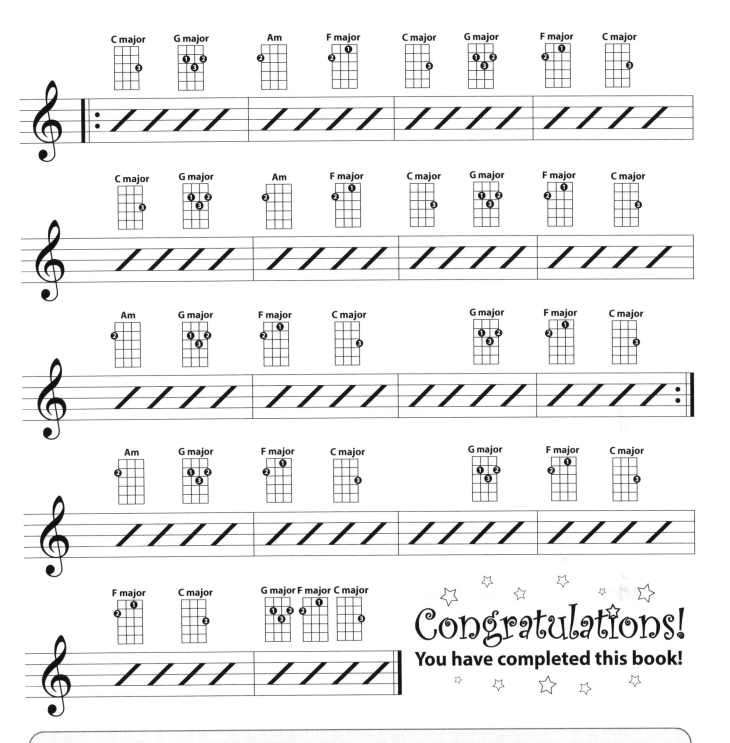

Don't Stop Here!

You've just learned a lot of new things about music and the ukulele. Now is a great time to:

☆ **Get your own ukulele, or get a nicer one.**
☆ **Find lead sheets for your favorite songs.**
☆ **Start a school ukulele club or a band.**
☆ **Experiment with chords to make your own songs.**
☆ **Learn how to play other instruments or practice singing.**

No matter what you choose, always keep learning and growing—**YOU** CAN DO IT!

Note Guide

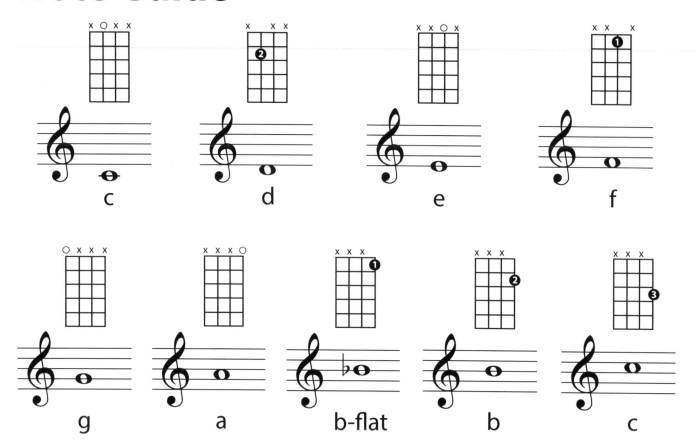

Chord Guide

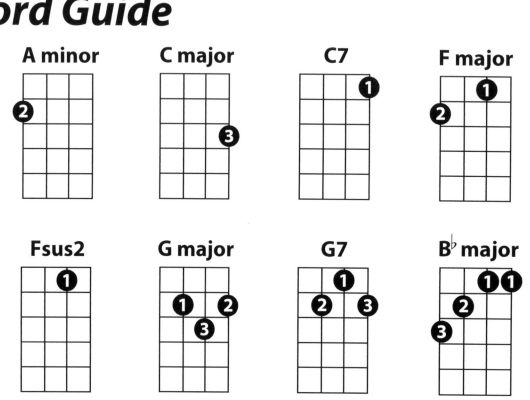

Song Index

Title (play-along recording artist), page	Chords	Melody	Lyrics	Play-Along
Aloha 'Oe, 48	✓	✓	✓	
Alouette, 46	✓	✓	✓	
Amazing Grace, 48-49	✓	✓	✓	
Bo Diddley (Bo Diddley), 34	✓			✓
Brahms' Lullaby, 42	✓	✓	✓	
Camptown Races, 29		✓	✓	
Coconut (Harry Nilsson), 24	✓			✓
Deep in the Heart of Texas (Moe Bandy), 33	✓			✓
Drifting Blues (B.B. King), 21	✓			✓
Duerme Pronto, 28		✓	✓	
Everybody Loves Saturday Night, 45	✓	✓	✓	
Exodus (Bob Marley), 27	✓			✓
Feelin' Alright (Joe Cocker), 26	✓			✓
Go Tell Aunt Rhody, 41	✓	✓	✓	
Happy Birthday to You, 47	✓			
Ho Hey (The Lumineers), 52-53	✓			✓
Home on the Range, 49-50	✓	✓	✓	
I Gotta Feeling, 27	✓			
Iko Iko (Cowboy Mouth), 33	✓			✓
Jambalaya (Hank Williams), 34	✓			✓
Lava (K.T. Kahele, N. Greig), 36	✓			✓
Let It Be (The Beatles), 54-55	✓			✓
London Bridge, 41	✓	✓	✓	
Merrily We Roll, 42	✓			
Mustang Sally (Wilson Pickett), 35	✓			✓
Rain, Rain, Go Away, 20		✓	✓	
Reggae Got Soul (311), 33	✓			✓
Ring Around the Rosie, 20		✓	✓	
Stand By Me, 27	✓			
Star Light, Star Bright, 20		✓	✓	
This Land Is Your Land (Flatt & Scruggs), 47	✓			✓
Twinkle, Twinkle, Little Star, 38		✓	✓	
When the Saints Go Marching In, 38	✓	✓	✓	
You Are My Sunshine (Willie Nelson), 47	✓			✓
You Can't Always Get What You Want (Rolling Stones), 26	✓			✓

Practice Record

Date	Assignment	Sun	Mon	Tue	Wed	Thu	Fri	Sat	Parent Initials